Early Land Owners Along the St. Vrain River, Nebraska and Colorado Territories

1858-1861

An Annotated Index

Compiled by Dina C. Carson

Early Land Owners Along the
St. Vrain River, Nebraska and
Colorado Territories,
1858-1861

An Annotated Index

Compiled by Dina C. Carson

Published by:

Iron Gate Publishing
P.O. Box 999
Niwot, CO 80544
www.irongate.com

Printed in the United States of America

ISBN   1-68224-006-1   ISBN 13   978-1-68224-006-9

Introduction

The *Early Land Owners Along the St. Vrain Creek, Colorado Territory, 1860-1861* is comprised of the recorded land records from four different sources of the same area and time period. Three of these sources are found in the Courthouse Collection of the Carnegie Branch Library for Local History in Boulder, Colorado. The collection is numbered 791 and these three items are found in Box 4, file folders 4, 5 and 6.

File Folder 4 holds the Record Book of Franklin Township Land Claims (along St Vrain Creek), 1860. This title is abbreviated as Franklin Township Land Claims in the text. This record book describes each claim in terms of its relationship to other local claims, and gives the direction and number of rods outlining the claim.

File Folder 5 holds the Record Book of Troy District Land Claims (along St Vrain Creek), 1861. This title is abbreviated as Troy District Land Claims in the text. These claims were recorded by Uri [Uriah] L. Peck and give both claims and preemptions. This record book describes each claim in terms of its relationship to other local claims, and gives the direction and number of rods outlining the claim.

File Folder 6 holds the Record Book of the St Vrain's Land Club's Land Claims, 1861. This title is abbreviated as St Vrain's Land Club Claims in the text. This record book includes land claims, sales and disputes. Each claim is described in terms of its relationship to other local claims, and gives the direction and number of rods outlining the claim.

The remaining source is in the archives of the Denver Public Library in the M687 Collection labeled Land Claim Association Records. This title is abbreviated as St Vrain County Land Claims in the text. These records are a typescript of original records held by the Weld County Board of County Commissioners office in Greeley. The first 49 pages are the land club records and are included here. The remaining 38 pages are the first records of the Board of County Commissioners for Weld County, Colorado Territory, and are not included as they do not pertain directly to land claims.

These original source documents are available for research through the respective repositories.

Abbreviations:

A number plus a capital letter "A" is shorthand for the number of acres claimed (i.e. 160A is 160 acres).

A

Adams

St Vrain's Land Club Claims
1860 Oct 29, pg 16, land mentioned in claim
1861 Jan 30, pg 10, land mentioned in claim
1861 Apr 11, pg 18, land mentioned in claim

Adams, R D

Franklin Township Land Claims
1860 June 25, pg 7, land mentioned in claim
1860 June 26, pg 6, claimant, at the NE corner of John Burch, 240A

St Vrain's Land Club Claims
1860 June 26, pg 17, claimant, 140A in Franklin Township, near John Burch's claim

Affolter, Fred

St Vrain's Land Club Claims
1861 Feb 18, pg 30, claimant, 320A, near Jessee Bloodworth's claim

Allen

Franklin Township Land Claims
1860 June 25, pg 6, land mentioned in claim

Allen, A N

Troy District Land Claims
1860 June 8, pg 13, land mentioned in claim
1860 July 5, pg 13, land mentioned in claim
1860 Dec 25, pg 19, land mentioned in claim

Allen, A P

St Vrain's Land Club Claims
1861 Feb 24, pg 32, agent
1861 Apr 7, pg 28, claimants, have built a dam, and commenced building a ditch with 14 square feet of running water, with each party entitled to water from the ditch
1861 Mar 5, pg 24, land mentioned in claim
1861 May 29, pg 3, Butler indenture to Allen & Dickens
1861 July 31, pg 5, [witness]

Allen, Nelson

St Vrain County Land Claims
1861 Jan 27, pg 31, witness

Anderson, Jonas

Troy District Land Claims
1861 Jan 29, pg 20, claimant, preemption, 160A, SE corner of G W Coffin's claim

Anderson, Jonas, cont.
1861 Mar 10, pg 10, re-signed claim to Thomas Dunn

Austan, J B
St Vrain's Land Club Claims
1861 Feb 18, pg 31, claimant, near C G Herington's claim

B

Bailey, L L
St Vrain County Land Claims
1861 Jan 25, pg 32, claimant, 160A

Baker, William
Franklin Township Land Claims
1860 Feb 11, pg 1, land mentioned in claim
1860 Feb 12, pg 3, land mentioned in claim
1860 Mar 10, pg 5, claimant, east of John T Burch, west of B A Franklin, 160A
St Vrain's Land Club Claims
1860 Feb 11, pg 16, land mentioned in claim

Baker, Wm
Franklin Township Land Claims
1860 Feb 12, pg 1, land mentioned in claim

Barber, J
St Vrain County Land Claims
1861 Mar 21, pg 41, witness

Barber, Oscar F
St Vrain County Land Claims
1861 Mar 21, pg 41, claimant, 160A, near J W Reddick's claim, staked 21 Mar 1861

Bass, P H
St Vrain's Land Club Claims
1861 May 6, pg 8, claimant, near Thomas McClane [McClain]

Bearman, James
St Vrain's Land Club Claims
[1861], pg 33, selling their claim to Thomas Read
[1861], pg 34, seller to Thomas Read

Beckwith
St Vrain's Land Club Claims
1861 Feb 24, pg 32, land mentioned in claim
1861 May 29, pg 4, land mentioned in claim

Beckwith (Sage & Beckwith)
Franklin Township Land Claims
1860 July 10, pg 5, claimants, near Jese [Jesse] Bloodsworth's SE corner

Beckwith, F C
St Vrain's Land Club Claims
   1861 Apr 7, pg 28, claimants, have built a dam,
   and commenced building
   a ditch with 14 square feet
   of running water, with
   each party entitled to
   water from the ditch

Beckwith, Frederick
St Vrain's Land Club Claims
   [1861], pg 33, land division,
   entry begun but crossed
   out

Beckwith, Frederick C
St Vrain's Land Club Claims
   1861 July 31, pg 5, claim
   dispute

Beckwith, Fredrick [Frederick]
St Vrain's Land Club Claims
   1861 Feb 16, pg 4, claim
   dispute

Beckwith, G L
St Vrain's Land Club Claims
   1861 Feb 24, pg 31, claimant
   1861 Apr 7, pg 28, claimants, have built a dam,
   and commenced building
   a ditch with 14 square feet
   of running water, with
   each party entitled to
   water from the ditch

   1861 May 29, pg 1, land
   mentioned in claim

Beckwith, George L
St Vrain's Land Club Claims
   1861 June 16, pg 5, records
   claim

Beckwith, L
St Vrain's Land Club Claims
   1861 Apr 7, pg 28, claimants, have built a dam,
   and commenced building
   a ditch with 14 square feet
   of running water, with
   each party entitled to
   water from the ditch

Beckwith, Lawson
St Vrain's Land Club Claims
   1861 May 29, pg 1, claimant, near G L Beckwith
   claim
   1861 July 24, pg 23, claimant, near William Butler's
   claim, near D C Powell's
   claim
   1861 July 24, pg 24, claimant, near William Butler's
   claim, near D C Powell's
   claim

Belcher
Troy District Land Claims
   1860 May 6, pg 16, land
   mentioned in claim
   1861 Jan 28, pg 11, land
   mentioned in claim

Belcher, Freeman
Troy District Land Claims
    1860 May 5, pg 16, claim-
    ant, preemption, 160A,
    SW corner of M H Cof-
    fin's claim
    1861 June 12, pg 1, house
    mentioned in claim

Bell, J W
Franklin Township Land Claims
    1860 July 6, pg 8, claimant,
    SW corner of John Weese

Berry, R
St Vrain County Land Claims
    1860 Apr 7, pg 16, witness

Bigalow, J E
St Vrain County Land Claims
    1859 Oct 13, pg 6, claimant,
    160A, near C E Miller's
    Claim, near James Pat-
    terson's claim, near Joseph
    How's claim, staked 13
    Oct 1859

Bloodsworth, Jese
Franklin Township Land Claims
    1860 July 10, pg 5, land
    mentioned in claim

Bloodworth
St Vrain's Land Club Claims
    1861 Mar 29, pg 25, land
    mentioned in claim

Bloodworth, Jessee [Jesse]
St Vrain's Land Club Claims
    [1861], pg 33, land division,
    entry begun but crossed
    out
    1861 Feb 16, pg 4, claim
    dispute
    1861 Feb 18, pg 30, land
    mentioned in claim
    1861 July 31, pg 5, claim
    dispute

Blower [Blore] & McCaslin
St Vrain's Land Club Claims
    1861 Sept 3, pg 22, claim
    surveyed, in Franklin
    Township, near Gwin's
    claim

Blower [Blore], W R
St Vrain's Land Club Claims
    1861 July 17, pg 22, claim
    surveyed, in Franklin
    Township, near Gwin's
    claim
    1861 Aug 29, pg 20, land
    mentioned in claim

Boughton, Ed
St Vrain County Land Claims
    1860 Nov 5, pg 27, Voter in
    the St Vrain Claim Club
    by residence

Boughton, M B
St Vrain County Land Claims
    1861 July 4, pg 47, witness

Boughton, M V
St Vrain County Land Claims
　1861 Apr 1, pg 42, agree-
　　ment to rates of any
　　future original shares
　　purchases
　1860 Apr 25, pg 15, witness
　1860 Nov 5, pg 27, Voter in
　　the St Vrain Claim Club
　　by residence

Bradford, R B
St Vrain County Land Claims
　1859 Oct 6, pg 1, Present
　　at the first meeting of the
　　Citizens of Saint Vrain

Bran, S
St Vrain's Land Club Claims
　1861 Nov 8, pg 39, claim-
　　ant, 160A, near Perry
　　White's claim

Brown, C R
Troy District Land Claims
　1861 Jan 28, pg 11, land
　　mentioned in claim

Brown, G A
St Vrain's Land Club Claims
　1861 Aug 18, pg 13, land
　　mentioned in claim

Brown, G P
St Vrain's Land Club Claims
　1861 Aug 14, pg 12, agent

Brown, George A
St Vrain's Land Club Claims
　1861 Aug 14, pg 11, claim-
　　ant, 160A, near James G
　　Ross's claim

Browne [Brown], C R
Troy District Land Claims
　1860 Oct 11, pg 21, witness
　1860 Dec 4, pg 22, claim-
　　ant, preemption, 160A,
　　SE corner of Uri L Peck's
　　claim
　1861 Jan 11, pg 8, land
　　mentioned in claim
　1861 Jan 26, pg 19, land
　　mentioned in claim
　1861 Oct 14, pg 7, land
　　mentioned in claim
　1860 Dec 5, pg 6, claimant,
　　preemption

Browne [Brown], Clark R
Troy District Land Claims
　1861 May 22, pg 6, lines
　　changed, along south fork
　　of the St Vrain Creek

Browne, Hiram T
Troy District Land Claims
　1861 Jan 11, pg 9, claimant,
　　preemption, 160A, SW
　　corner of C R Browne's
　　claim

Bruce

St Vrain's Land Club Claims
1861 Aug 22, pg 19, land
mentioned in claim

Bruce, Jacob

St Vrain's Land Club Claims
1861 Feb 16, pg 32, land
mentioned in claim
1861 July 31, pg 5, refrey
[referee] to land dispute
1861 Aug 11, pg 14, land
mentioned in claim
1861 Aug 11, pg 14, land
mentioned in claim
1861 Aug 14, pg 11, land
mentioned in claim
1861 Aug 28, pg 20, land
mentioned in claim
1862 Jan 11, pg 39, land
mentioned in claim

Burbridge, Charles W

St Vrain County Land Claims
1864 Dec 1, pg , brand filed
with the Weld County
Clerk

Burch, John

Franklin Township Land Claims
1860 June 26, pg 6, land
mentioned in claim
St Vrain's Land Club Claims
1860 June 26, pg 17, land
mentioned in claim

Burch, John T

Franklin Township Land Claims
1860 Feb 11, pg 1, claimant,
corner of William Baker
Claim, 320A
1860 Feb 15, pg 3, land
mentioned in claim
St Vrain's Land Club Claims
1860 Feb 11, pg 16, claimant, near William Baker's
claim
1860 Feb 15, pg 16, land
mentioned in claim
1861 Sept 8, pg 26, claimants, land known as the
Bruce claim, near H
Goodwin, near James G
Ross
1861 Sept 8, pg 42, [wit-
ness]

Burtch, John

Franklin Township Land Claims
1860 June 29, pg 8, land
mentioned in claim

Butler, Helen

St Vrain's Land Club Claims
1861 May 29, pg 3, wife of
William E Butler, of Co-
lumbus Co., WI
1861 May 29, pg 4, party to
the land sale

Butler, W E
St Vrain's Land Club Claims
    1861 Apr 7, pg 28, claimants, have built a dam, and commenced building a ditch with 14 square feet of running water, with each party entitled to water from the ditch

Butler, William
St Vrain's Land Club Claims
    1861 July 24, pg 23, land mentioned in claim

Butler, William E
St Vrain's Land Club Claims
    1861 Feb 24, pg 32, claimant, 160A, near William H Dickens, on Left Hand Creek, near Beckwith's claim
    1861 May 29, pg 3, Butler indenture to Allen & Dickens, of Columbus Co., WI
    1861 May 29, pg 4, party to the land sale

Byers, W T
St Vrain County Land Claims
    1859 Oct 12, pg 11, claimant, 160A, near the Town of Saint Vrain, near Geo French's claim, claimed 12 Oct 1859

    1860 Feb 21, pg 11, seller, of Arapahoe County, Kansas Territory, quit claim deed to Ellen D Graham

Byers, William T
St Vrain County Land Claims
    1860 Feb 21, pg 12, appeared before a Notary Public in Arapahoe County, Kansas Territory

Byers, Wm T
St Vrain County Land Claims
    1859 Oct 6, pg 1, Present at the first meeting of the Citizens of Saint Vrain
    1860 Feb 21, pg 12, seller, quit claim deed to Ellen D Graham

C

Calderbank, Wm
Troy District Land Claims
    1861 July 29, pg 2, claimant, preemption, 160A, SE corner of Theophilus Taylor claim

Calhuen, C B
St Vrain's Land Club Claims
    1861 Aug 18, pg 15, claimant, near D C Powell's claim

Calhuen, W W
St Vrain's Land Club Claims
1861 Aug 18, pg 15, claimant, near D C Powell's claim

Carden, John
Franklin Township Land Claims
1860 June 26, pg 7, claimant, corner of Wm Baker

Carpe, *see Corpe*

Carpe, L
St Vrain County Land Claims
1860 Oct 23, pg 24, committee to read the resolution to vacate to the trespassers

Carpe, Lincoln
St Vrain County Land Claims
1860 Nov 5, pg 27, Voter in the St Vrain Claim Club by residence

Carpe, Simeon
St Vrain County Land Claims
1860 Dec 6, pg 30, claimant, 160A, near John H Overton's claim

Carter (Taylor & Carter)
St Vrain's Land Club Claims
1861 Apr 7, pg 28, claimants, have built a dam, and commenced building a ditch with 14 square feet

of running water, with each party entitled to water from the ditch

Carter, C
St Vrain's Land Club Claims
1861 Feb 16, pg 4, [role unclear]

Carter, John
St Vrain's Land Club Claims
1860 June 26, pg 18, claimant, near Mr Baker's claim

Cartwright
St Vrain's Land Club Claims
1860 Feb 1, pg 17, land mentioned in claim
1860 Feb 15, pg 16, land mentioned in claim

Cassity, John
St Vrain County Land Claims
1860 May 10, pg 18, claimant, 160A, near Wm Scourfield's claim, staked 10 May 1860

Castle, W W
St Vrain County Land Claims
1859 Oct 12, pg 3, claimant, 160A, staked 12 Oct 1859

Cawkins [Hawkins]
St Vrain County Land Claims
1860 Oct 23, pg 21, in a dispute with H J Graham over a claim

Cawkins [Hawkins], Hiram
St Vrain County Land Claims
1861 Mar 1, pg 37, claim,
160A

Ceeman, Jeremiah
St Vrain County Land Claims
1861 May 8, pg 45, claimant, 160A

Ceenan
St Vrain County Land Claims
1860 Oct 23, pg 21, in a dispute with H J Graham over a claim

Ceenan, J
St Vrain County Land Claims
1861 May 8, pg 46, witness

Ceenan, Jeremiah
St Vrain County Land Claims
1860 Oct 23, pg 24, trespassing on the claim of H J Graham

Ceenen
St Vrain County Land Claims
1860 Oct 23, pg 25, notice to vacate

Charles, John Q
Troy District Land Claims
1860 Oct 4, pg 18, witness

Clifton, William
St Vrain's Land Club Claims
1861 Mar 5, pg 24, claimant, near the Laramie

Road, on the Little Thompson

Clifton, Wm
St Vrain's Land Club Claims
1861 Mar 5, pg 24, land mentioned in claim

Coffin
Troy District Land Claims
1861 Jan 28, pg 11, land mentioned in claim

Coffin, G W
Troy District Land Claims
1860 June 18, pg 17, claimant, preemption, 160A, SE corner of M H Coffin's claim
1860 Aug 10, pg 17, claimant, preemption renewed
1860 Oct 26, pg 22, land mentioned in claim
1861 Jan 29, pg 20, land mentioned in claim
1861 Apr 30, pg 4, land mentioned in claim

Coffin, M H
Troy District Land Claims
1860 June 18, pg 17, land mentioned in claim
1860 May 4, pg 1, claimant, preemption
1860 May 5, pg 16, land mentioned in claim

Coffin, M H, cont.

1860 May 6, pg 16, claimant, preemption, 160A, SE corner Belcher's claim

1860 Aug 10, pg 1, claim renewed

1860 Aug 10, pg 16, claimant, preemption renewed

1861 June 12, pg 1, lines changed

1861 June 22, pg 1, claimant

Collier, D C

St Vrain County Land Claims

1860 Feb 21, pg 12, Notary Public for Arapahoe County, Kansas Territory

1860 Feb 21, pg 12, witness

Conerickly?, A P

St Vrain's Land Club Claims

1861 May 17, pg 2, claimant, 160A, near H C King's claim

Connolly, C M

St Vrain County Land Claims

1859 Oct 28, pg 7, witness

Connolly, Charles M

St Vrain County Land Claims

1860 Apr 25, pg 15, seller, quit claim deed to George French

1860 Apr 30, pg 14, claimant, staked 15 Sept 1859

Cook, Dr

St Vrain County Land Claims

1859 Oct 6, pg 1, Present at the first meeting of the Citizens of Saint Vrain

Copse

St Vrain County Land Claims

1861 Feb 16, pg 34, land mentioned in a claim

Corpe

St Vrain County Land Claims

1861 May 8, pg 46, buyer, for $10, land near John Wogin's claim

Corpe, Simeon

St Vrain County Land Claims

1861 Jan 10, pg 39, witness

1861 May 8, pg 45, witness

1861 May 8, pg 46, seller, land to Corpe [no first name given]

Craig, John H

St Vrain County Land Claims

1860 Apr 7, pg 16, witness

Cronk, David

Troy District Land Claims

1860 Oct 6, pg 17, claimant, preemption, 160A, W of J G Robinson's original NE corner

Cronk, George
Troy District Land Claims
> 1861 Feb 19, pg 8, claimant, preemption, 160A, SE corner of Rufus Rice's claim
> 1861 July 9, pg 2, lines changed, beginning SE corner of Rufus Rice's claim
> 1862 Feb 19, pg 2, claimant, preemption

Crook, R
Franklin Township Land Claims
> 1860 June 24, pg 7, land mentioned in claim

Crook, R C & Co
Franklin Township Land Claims
> 1860 June 25, pg 6, claimant, near SW corner of Hoover and Wagoner's land, 160A

Culver, Cary
St Vrain's Land Club Claims
> 1861 Aug 27, pg 21, claimant, near Robert Culver's claim

Culver, Robert
St Vrain's Land Club Claims
> 1861 Aug 27, pg 21, land mentioned in claim
> 1861 Aug 27, pg 21, claimant, near T D McClain's claim

> 1861 Aug 29, pg 22, land mentioned in claim

Cunningham, Owen
St Vrain County Land Claims
> 1861 May 3, pg 43, witness

Cushman, A
St Vrain's Land Club Claims
> 1861 Apr 19, pg 37, notice of land dispute between A Cushman and W Mead, near Goodwin's claim
> 1861 Apr 24, pg 35, selling 1/2 his claim to N Cushman

Cushman, Alfred
St Vrain's Land Club Claims
> [1861 Mar 29], pg 25, claimants, land purchased by Mead & Co of Jessee Bloodworth on 25 Sept 1860 for $80

Cushman, N
St Vrain's Land Club Claims
> 1861 Apr 24, pg 35, buying a portion of a claim from A Cushman

Cutler, Porter
St Vrain County Land Claims
> 1864 Dec 10, pg , brand filed with the Weld County Clerk

D

Dalton, Patrick
  St Vrain County Land Claims
    1859 Dec 15, pg 10, claimant, 160A, near Fort Lupton, recorded 10 Jan 1860, staked and marked 15 Dec 1859

Daniel, H
  Troy District Land Claims
    1861 Jan 28, pg 11, land mentioned in claim

Daniel, Henry
  Troy District Land Claims
    1861 Jan 28, pg 12, land mentioned in claim

Darclone, Thomas
  St Vrain's Land Club Claims
    1861 Aug 15, pg 15, land mentioned in claim

Davis, Mahlon
  St Vrain's Land Club Claims
    1861 Mar 25, pg 26, claimant, near Louis Stone's claim
    1861 Apr 5, pg 23, land mentioned in claim

Day, Elizabeth
  St Vrain's Land Club Claims
    1861 Feb 2, pg 10, claimant, near Aaron Runian [Runyon]'s claim, on the Laramie Road
    1861 Dec 1, pg 38, claimant, 160A, near Thomas Mc-Clain's claim
    1861 Dec 1, pg 38, land mentioned in claim

Denver and Fort Laramie Road
  St Vrain's Land Club Claims
    1861 June 16, pg 8, road mentioned in claim

Dickens, Allen G
  St Vrain's Land Club Claims
    1861 Mar 5, pg 24, claimant, near A P Allen's claim, near W H Dickens's claim

Dickens, W H
  St Vrain's Land Club Claims
    1861 Mar 5, pg 24, land mentioned in claim
    1861 Apr 7, pg 28, claimants, have built a dam, and commenced building a ditch with 14 square feet of running water, with each party entitled to water from the ditch
    1861 May 29, pg 3, Butler indenture to Allen & Dickens
    1861 May 29, pg 4, land mentioned in claim

Dickens, William H
St Vrain's Land Club Claims
    1861 Feb 24, pg 32, land
    mentioned in claim

Dickson, Lewis H
Troy District Land Claims
    1861 Apr 9, pg 5, claimant,
    preemption, 160A, near G
    W Coffin's SE corner

Dunham, S
Franklin Township Land Claims
    1860 June 24, pg 7, claim-
    ant, near R Crook, 160A

Dunham, Wright
Troy District Land Claims
    1860 Aug 3, pg 15, claim-
    ant, preemption, 160A,
    SE corner of N D Parker's
    claim

Dunn, Thomas
Troy District Land Claims
    1861 Jan 28, pg 11, claim-
    ant, near SE corner of
    Belcher's claim, SW cor-
    ner of C R Brown's claim,
    W of H Daniel's claim, S
    of Robinson's claim, E of
    Coffin's claim
    1861 Jan 31, pg 12, witness
    1861 Mar 10, pg 10, claim-
    ant, along St Vrains Creek
    1861 Apr 30, pg 4, land
    mentioned in claim

Dunstan, E
St Vrain's Land Club Claims
    1861 July 31, pg 5, [witness]

Dunstan, J H R
St Vrain's Land Club Claims
    1861 July 31, pg 5, [witness]

Dunstan, John H R
Troy District Land Claims
    1860 July 5, pg 13, claim-
    ant, preemption, 160A,
    SE corner of A N Allen's
    claim
    1860 July 17, pg 14, land
    mentioned in claim
    1861 Mar 22, pg 10, land
    mentioned in claim

Dunston, Thomas
St Vrain's Land Club Claims
    1861 July 31, pg 5, refrey
    [referee] to land dispute

Dwight & Penick [Pennock]
St Vrain's Land Club Claims
    1861 Jan 30, pg 10, claim-
    ant, 160A, known as the
    Adams claim, near G E
    Gubins

Dwight & Pennock
St Vrain's Land Club Claims
    1861 Jan 30, pg 10, claim-
    ant, 160A, known as the
    Adams claim, near G E
    Gubins

Dwight (Penock [Pennock] & Dwight)

St Vrain's Land Club Claims
    1861 Apr 11, pg 18, sellers to C C True and G W Webster

E

Ebi, Daniel/David

St Vrain's Land Club Claims
    1862 Jan 11, pg 39, claimant, 160A, near Jacob Bruce's claim

Elison, Daniel

St Vrain's Land Club Claims
    1861 June 16, pg 7, notary public, of Montgomery Co., IA

Elliot, James

St Vrain's Land Club Claims
    1861 Aug 15, pg 15, claimant, 640A, near Thomas Darclone?'s claim

Emerick, A J

St Vrain's Land Club Claims
    1861 May 18, pg 36, claimant, 160A, near H C King's claim

F

Finney, F

St Vrain County Land Claims
    1861 Mar 15, pg 38, witness
    1861 Mar 15, pg 39, claimant, 160A near Geo Lyche's claim

Finney, Franklin

St Vrain County Land Claims
    [1861 Mar], pg 41, seller, quit claim to Michal Smith and Andrew H Smith

Flack, A J

St Vrain County Land Claims
    1861 Apr 3, pg 43, witness

Fleming, George A

St Vrain County Land Claims
    1861 July 4, pg 47, buyer, land from Frank Reynolds and James Francis, for $950 and 1 black pony, 3 milch cows, 3 sythes and sneds, one grindstone, 1 pig, 3 wagons, 5 log chains, 3 ox yokes and the bridge.

Flemming, Geo

St Vrain County Land Claims
    1861 Aug 24, pg 48, land mentioned in a claim

Fletcher, Chandler
Franklin Township Land Claims
1860 May 25, pg 6, claimant, north side St Vrain Creek

Fletcher, John
Franklin Township Land Claims
1860 May 25, pg 6, claimant, north side St Vrain Creek

Fort Laramie Road
St Vrain's Land Club Claims
1861 Feb 2, pg 10, road mentioned in claim

Fort Lupton
St Vrain County Land Claims
1859 Dec 15, pg 10, fort mentioned in a claim

Fort Saint Vrain
St Vrain County Land Claims
1860 Nov 5, pg 28, fort mentioned in a claim
1861 Jan 10, pg 39, fort mentioned in a claim

Fort Vasquez
St Vrain County Land Claims
1859 Oct 28, pg 7, fort mentioned in a claim

Francis, James
St Vrain County Land Claims
1861 Jan 18, pg 40, witness

1861 Feb 21, pg 37, claimant, near the J H Overton claim bought by B F Reynolds, near John Wogin's claim
1861 July 4, pg 47, seller, two claims known as the Overton claims, near Irish Johnny's claim, and two claims known as the Reynolds and Francis claims, to George A Fleming
1861 Aug 24, pg 48, buyer, quit claim from B F Reynolds, between the Overton and John Wogin's claims

Franklin, B A
Franklin Township Land Claims
1860 Feb 12, pg 1, land mentioned in claim
1860 Feb 12, pg 2, land mentioned in claim
1860 Feb 12, pg 3, claimant, NW corner of William Baker, 160A

French, Geo
St Vrain County Land Claims
1859 Oct 12, pg 11, land mentioned in a claim
1860 Jan 7, pg 9, land mentioned in a claim
1860 Apr 9, pg 17, witness

French, Geo, cont.

> 1860 Oct 23, pg 21, Present at a meeting of the Citizens of St Vrain, appointed to the committee to examin[e] the record of the organized club of St Vrain County

> 1860 Oct 23, pg 22, gave a resolution showing that a person or persons had cut large amounts of timber and had errected a cabin on the claim of H J Graham, one of the oldest citizen residents of the county

> 1860 Oct 23, pg 25, Present at a meeting of the Saint Vrain Claim Club, elected president

> 1860 Oct 23, pg 25, Present at a meeting of the Saint Vrain Claim Club, appointed to a committee to draft rules and laws

> 1860 Nov 5, pg 26, Present at a meeting of the St Vrain Claim Club

> 1860 Nov 5, pg 27, Voter in the St Vrain Claim Club by residence

> 1860 Nov 5, pg 27, president

> 1861 Jan 12, pg 30, buyer, for $150, quit claim from Ellen D and H J Graham

French, George

St Vrain County Land Claims

> 1859 Oct, pg 9, claimant, 160A, claimed Oct 1859, staked and improved 7 Jan 1860

> 1860 Feb 21, pg 12, land mentioned in a claim

> 1860 Apr 25, pg 15, buyer, for $100, quit claim deed from Charles M Connolly

G

Gaines, Richard

Franklin Township Land Claims

> 1860 Feb 15, pg 3, land mentioned in claim

Gardner, C H

Troy District Land Claims

> 1861 Jan 26, pg 19, claimant, preemption, 160A, SW corner of C R Brown's

Gardner, John

St Vrain County Land Claims

> 1861 May 21, pg 44, claimant, near the Saint Vrain Town Site, near Grahm's claim

Gardner, William
St Vrain's Land Club Claims
  1861 Aug 29, pg 22, claimant, 160A, near Robert
  Culver's claim

Gersiwald, E S
St Vrain's Land Club Claims
  1861 Apr 29, pg 4, notary
  public, of Columbus Co.,
  WI
  1861 May 29, pg 4, witness

Gifford, A D
St Vrain's Land Club Claims
  1861 Aug 11, pg 14, claimant, of Franklin Township,
  160A, 1/2 mile south of
  Jacob Bruce's claim filed
  on 28 June 1860

Goodwin
St Vrain's Land Club Claims
  1861 Apr 19, pg 37, land
  mentioned in claim

Goodwin, H
St Vrain's Land Club Claims
  1861 Mar 20, pg 28, land
  mentioned in claim
  1861 June 23, pg 9, land
  mentioned in claim
  1861 July 29, pg 11, land
  mentioned in claim
  1861 Aug 22, pg 19, land
  mentioned in claim
  [1861], pg 33, land mentioned in claim

Goodwin, H (Dr)
St Vrain's Land Club Claims
  1861 May 23, pg 41, land
  mentioned in claim
  1861 May 26, pg 2, land
  mentioned in claim

Goodwin, Harrison
Franklin Township Land Claims
  1860 June 24, pg 5, land
  mentioned in claim

Grafflin, Wm H
St Vrain County Land Claims
  1865 Feb 9, pg , brand filed
  with the Weld County
  Clerk

Graham, Ellen D
St Vrain County Land Claims
  1860 Feb 21, pg 11, pur-
  chaser, quit claim deed
  from W T Byers for $50
  1861 Jan 12, pg 30, seller,
  quit claim to Geo French

Graham, Ellen D (Mrs)
St Vrain County Land Claims
  1860 Jan 7, pg 9, claimant,
  160A, near the Town of
  Saint Vrain, near Geo
  French's claim, staked,
  marked and improved 7
  and 9 Jan 1860.

Graham, H J

St Vrain County Land Claims

1858 Nov 1, pg 18, witness

1859 July 21, pg 2, claimant, near S H Moer's claim, staked 21 July 1859, renewed 30 Sept 1859, work done 12 Oct 1859, recorded at Denver City, July 1859

1859 July 21, pg 2, witness

1859 Sept 30, pg 2, land mentioned in a claim

[1859 Oct], pg 5, purchase, 80A from C P Neall for $50, claimant additional 80A, near the Saint Vrain Town Site, improved 15 May 1860

1859 Oct, pg 9, witness

1859 Oct 6, pg 1, Present at the first meeting of the Citizens of Saint Vrain, chosen Secretary

1860 Jan 7, pg 9, witness

1860 Mar 5, pg 14, recorder

1860 May 10, pg 18, witness

1860 Oct 23, pg 21, Present at a meeting of the Citizens of St Vrain

1860 Oct 23, pg 21, declared the rightful owner of Claim No. 10

1860 Oct 23, pg 22, had had his claim violated by a person or persons who had cut down a large amount of timber to build a cabin

1860 Oct 23, pg 23, the Citizens of Saint Vrain pledge themselves to help uphold the claim of H J Graham

1860 Oct 23, pg 25, Present at a meeting of the Saint Vrain Claim Club, resigned and then re-elected as recorder

1860 Nov 5, pg 26, Present at a meeting of the St Vrain Claim Club

1860 Nov 5, pg 27, recorder

1860 Nov 5, pg 27, Voter in the St Vrain Claim Club by residence

1860 Nov 12, pg 29, witness

1861 Jan 12, pg 30, seller, quit claim to Geo French

1861 Jan 15, pg 40, witness

1861 Feb 4, pg 33, recorder, recorded the claim of D J Hopkins under protest as the land is a part of the Town of Saint Vrain

1861 Feb 16, pg 35, witness

1861 Feb 16, pg 36, witness

1861 Feb 21, pg 37, recorder

1861 Mar 1, pg 37, recorder, recorded the claim of Hiram Cawkins under protest as the land is a

part of the Town of Saint
Vrain
1861 Mar 15, pg 38, witness
1861 Mar 15, pg 38, witness
1861 Mar 15, pg 39, witness
1861 Apr 1, pg 42, agree-
  ment to rates of any
  future original shares
  purchases
1861 Apr 3, pg 43, witness
1861 May 8, pg 45, witness
1861 May 8, pg 46, witness
1861 Aug 24, pg 48, witness
1862 [1861] Feb 16, pg 36,
  witness

Graham, Hiram J
St Vrain County Land Claims
  1860 Mar 5, pg 13, buyer,
  for $50, quit claim deed
  from Corydore P Neall,
  near the Town of Saint
  Vrain,
  1860 Oct, pg 20, recorder
  1861 May 10, pg 49, seller,
  land in the Town of Saint
  Vrain to J W Reddick

Graham, T J
St Vrain's Land Club Claims
  1861 Aug 18, pg 13, claimant, near G A Brown's
  claim

Grant, Edward
Franklin Township Land Claims
  1860 Feb 16, pg 4, agent for
  Luman Read
St Vrain's Land Club Claims
  1860 Feb 1, pg 17, agent

Griffith, Edward W
Franklin Township Land Claims
  1860 Feb 15, pg 3, agent for
  Jonathan Troxel
St Vrain's Land Club Claims
  1860 Feb 15, pg 17, agent

Gubins, G E
St Vrain's Land Club Claims
  1861 Jan 30, pg 10, land
  mentioned in claim

Guinn
Franklin Township Land Claims
  1860 Feb 11, pg 1, land
  mentioned in claim

Guinn, T
Franklin Township Land Claims
  1860 Feb 20, pg 4, claimant,
  320A

Gwin
St Vrain's Land Club Claims
  1860 Oct 29, pg 16, land
  mentioned in claim
  1861 July 17, pg 22, land
  mentioned in claim

Gwin, G C
St Vrain's Land Club Claims
1861 Apr 11, pg 18, land
mentioned in claim

Gwin, Richard
St Vrain's Land Club Claims
1860 Feb 15, pg 16, land
mentioned in claim

H

Hartgrove, Nelson
St Vrain's Land Club Claims
1861 Apr 5, pg 23, claimant,
near Mahlon Davis's claim

Hartgrove, William
St Vrain's Land Club Claims
1861 Apr 8, pg 23, claimant,
near N Teater's claim

Hawkins
St Vrain County Land Claims
1860 Oct 23, pg 25, notice
to vacate

Hawkins, Hiram
St Vrain County Land Claims
1860 Oct 23, pg 24, tres-
passing on the claim of H
J Graham

Henderson, Joseph
Franklin Township Land Claims
1860 June 24, pg 5, land
mentioned in claim

1860 June 24, pg 5, claimant, SE corner of Harrison
Goodwin

Heriman, A
St Vrain's Land Club Claims
1861 Apr 11, pg 29, claimant, near G B Stanley,
with the consent of G S
Runian

Herington, C G
St Vrain's Land Club Claims
1861 Feb 18, pg 31, land
mentioned in claim
1861 Feb 18, pg 31, claimant, near T D McClain's
claim

Hill, Miles
St Vrain's Land Club Claims
1861 Mar 29, pg 27, claimant, near Thomas Reed's
claim
1861 Apr 1, pg 27, land
mentioned in claim
1861 Apr 20, pg 34, land
mentioned in claim

Hill, Sylvester
St Vrain's Land Club Claims
1861 Aug 19, pg 12, claimant, near the Waterloo
town cite [sic]

Hollingshead, Thomas
St Vrain County Land Claims
  1861 Apr 15, pg 44, claimant, 160A, near V Mogle's
  claim,
  1861 Apr 15, pg 45, seller,
  land to V Mogle

Hollowell, J W
St Vrain's Land Club Claims
  1861 Nov 28, pg 43, of
  Thompson Creek, Colo-
  rado Territory, buys land
  from Perry White

Holmess, A
St Vrain County Land Claims
  1860 Oct 23, pg 24, committee to read the resolution to vacate to the
  trespassers

Hoover, D C
Franklin Township Land Claims
  1860 June 25, pg 6, claimant, below Allen's claim,
  160A

Hoover, R C & Co
Franklin Township Land Claims
  1860 June 25, pg 6, signa-
  ture [the top of the listing
  says R C Crook & Co]

Hopkins, D J
St Vrain County Land Claims
  1861 Feb 4, pg 32, claimant, 160A, near Albert

Thorn's claim, staked and
improved 4 Feb 1861

Hopkins, W L
St Vrain County Land Claims
  1859 Oct 22, pg 7, claimant,
  160A, near Joseph How's
  claim, staked 22 Oct 1859.

Hopkins, Wm L
Troy District Land Claims
  1860 Dec 25, pg 19, claimant, preemption, 160A,
  SE corner of A N Allen's
  claim

How, Joseph
St Vrain County Land Claims
  1859 Oct 12, pg 6, claimant,
  160A, near C E Miller's
  claim, staked 12 Oct 1859
  1859 Oct 13, pg 6, land
  mentioned in a claim

I

Irish Johnny
St Vrain County Land Claims
  1861 July 4, pg 47, land
  mentioned in a claim

J

James, G
St Vrain's Land Club Claims
1861 June 23, pg 9, land
mentioned in claim

James, Gilbert
St Vrain's Land Club Claims
1861 Feb 16, pg 9, claimant,
near William Meek and H
E King

Johnson, H
St Vrain's Land Club Claims
1861 July 29, pg 11, claimant, 160A, near H Good-
win's claim

Jones, J Y
St Vrain County Land Claims
1859 Sept 30, pg 2, claimant, near H J Graham's
claim, staked 30 Sept 1859
1859 Sept 30, pg 3, land
mentioned in a claim
1859 Oct 6, pg 1, Present
at the first meeting of the
Citizens of Saint Vrain
1859 Oct 13, pg 6, land
mentioned in a claim

Jones, John W
St Vrain County Land Claims
1859 Sept 9, pg 4, claim-
ant, 160A, near C P Neill's
claim, staked 9 Sept 1859

K

King, H C
St Vrain's Land Club Claims
1861 May 16, pg 35, claimant, 160A, near Thomas
McClain's claim
1861 May 17, pg 2, land
mentioned in claim
1861 May 18, pg 36, land
mentioned in claim

King, H E
St Vrain's Land Club Claims
1861 Feb 15, pg 30, claimant, 160A, near T D Mc-
Clain's claim
1861 Feb 16, pg 9, land
mentioned in claim

L

Lamberson, A
St Vrain County Land Claims
1861 Apr 3, pg 43, claimant,
160A, claimed 2 Feb 1861,
recorded 3 Apr 1861

Laramie Road
St Vrain's Land Club Claims
1861 Mar 5, pg 24, road
mentioned in claim

Larwing?, Harley
St Vrain's Land Club Claims
1861 May 29, pg 4, witness

Latham, G C
St Vrain's Land Club Claims
1861 Apr 17, pg 28,
claimant, near Runian
[Runyon]'s claim

Latto, J A
St Vrain's Land Club Claims
1861 Aug 15, pg 15, claimant, 640A, near Thomas
Darclone?'s claim

Latto, S G
St Vrain's Land Club Claims
1861 Aug 15, pg 15, claimant, 640A, near Thomas
Darclone?'s claim

Lewis, Wm
Troy District Land Claims
1861 Mar 22, pg 10, claim-
ant, preemption, 160A,
SE corner of John H B
Dunstan

Louders, Peter J
St Vrain County Land Claims
1861 July 4, pg 47, witness

Low [Lowe], R S
St Vrain's Land Club Claims
1861 Aug 19, pg 12, claimant, near Andrew M
Powell claim
1861 Aug 19, pg 13, land
mentioned in claim

Lowe, P G
St Vrain County Land Claims
1859 Oct 6, pg 1, Present
at the first meeting of the
Citizens of Saint Vrain

Lyche, Geo
St Vrain County Land Claims
1861 Mar 15, pg 39, land
mentioned in a claim

M

Maris, Herbert
St Vrain's Land Club Claims
[1861], pg 33, claimant,
near H Goodwin's claim,
near William Meek's
claim

Mason, William S
Franklin Township Land Claims
1860 Feb 11, pg 1, claimant,
north of Guinn and Mc-
Cun's claim, 160A

Matthews [Mathews], Orson
St Vrain's Land Club Claims
[1861], pg 34, witness

McBride, R E
St Vrain's Land Club Claims
1861 Dec 1, pg 38, claim-
ants, 160A, near Elizabeth
Day's claim

McCall, Thomas
Franklin Township Land Claims
1860 June 25, pg 7, claimant, east of R D Adams
1860 June 29, pg 8, claimant, on east line of John
Burch

**McCaslin (Blower [Blore] & Mc-
Caslin)**
St Vrain's Land Club Claims
1861 Sept 3, pg 22, claim
surveyed, in Franklin
Township, near Gwin's
claim

McCaslin, M L
St Vrain's Land Club Claims
1861 July 17, pg 22, claim
surveyed, in Franklin
Township, near Gwin's
claim

McClain, T D
St Vrain's Land Club Claims
1861 Feb 15, pg 30, land
mentioned in claim
1861 Feb 18, pg 31, land
mentioned in claim
1861 May 17, pg 36, land
mentioned in claim
1861 Aug 22, pg 19, claimant, land known as the
Bruce claim, near H
Goodwin's claim
1861 Aug 27, pg 21, land
mentioned in claim

1861 Aug 27, pg 21, land
mentioned in claim
1861 Aug 29, pg 20, land
mentioned in claim

McClain, Thomas
St Vrain's Land Club Claims
1861 May 16, pg 35, land
mentioned in claim
1861 June 16, pg 8, land
mentioned in claim
1861 Sept 8, pg 42, land
mentioned in claim
1861 Dec 1, pg 38, land
mentioned in claim
1862, Jan 26, pg 40, land
mentioned in claim

McClain, Thomas D
St Vrain's Land Club Claims
1861 May 20, pg 37, claimant, 160A, near G Tower's
claim

McClane [McClain], Thomas
St Vrain's Land Club Claims
1861 May 6, pg 8, land
mentioned in claim

McCun
Franklin Township Land Claims
1860 Feb 11, pg 1, land
mentioned in claim

Mcelany?, Wm
St Vrain's Land Club Claims
1861 Aug 15, pg 15, claim-

ant, 640A, near Thomas Darclone?'s claim

McGeen, John H
St Vrain's Land Club Claims
1861 Mar 5, pg 24, claimant, near Wm Clifton's claim, on the Little Thompson

McManus, Denis
St Vrain County Land Claims
1861 May 21, pg 44, claimant, near the Saint Vrain Town Site, near Grahm's claim

McMillin, J W
St Vrain's Land Club Claims
1861 June 1, pg 1, claimant, 160A

McWade, James
St Vrain County Land Claims
1859 Oct 25, pg 8, claimant, 160A, staked 25 Oct 1859

Mead, W
St Vrain's Land Club Claims
1861 Apr 19, pg 37, notice of land dispute between A Cushman and W Mead, near Goodwin's claim

Mead, William
St Vrain's Land Club Claims
[1861 Mar 29], pg 25, claimants, land purchased by Mead & Co of Jessee Bloodworth on 25 Sept 1860 for $80
1861 Mar 29, pg 25, claimant, land known as the Bloodworth claim, purchased by William Mead on 29 Sept 1860 from Bloodworth for $80

Meek, William
Franklin Township Land Claims
1860 June 24, pg 5, claimant, SW corner of Joseph Henderson, 160A
St Vrain's Land Club Claims
1861 Feb 16, pg 9, land mentioned in claim
1861 Mar 20, pg 27, claimant, near H Goodwin's claim
[1861], pg 33, land mentioned in claim

Miller, C E
St Vrain County Land Claims
1859 Sept 30, pg 3, claimant, 160A, near J Y Jones's claim, staked 30 Sept 1859
1859 Oct 6, pg 1, Present at the first meeting of the Citizens of Saint Vrain
1859 Oct 13, pg 6, land mentioned in a claim

Miller, James B

St Vrain County Land Claims
1861 July 4, pg 46, claimant, 160A, claimed 17 June 1861, recorded 4 July 1861

Mitchell, S F

St Vrain County Land Claims
1861 May 3, pg 42, seller, of Arapahoe County, Colorado Territory, quit claim to John J Lanille
1861 May 3, pg 43, seller

Moer, S H

St Vrain County Land Claims
1859 July 21, pg 2, land mentioned in a claim
1859 July 21, pg 2, claimant, staked 21 July 1859, renewed 30 Sept 1859, work done 12 Oct 1859, recorded at Denver City, July 1859
1859 Sept 30, pg 3, witness
1859 Sept 30, pg 3, witness
1859 Oct 12, pg 3, witness
1859 Oct 12, pg 4, witness
1859 Oct 12, pg 5, witness
1859 Oct 12, pg 5, witness
1859 Oct 12, pg 6, witness
1859 Oct 22, pg 7, witness
1859 Oct 25, pg 8, witness

Mogel, Valentine

St Vrain County Land Claims
1860 Nov 5, pg 28, witness
1860 Nov 11, pg 28, claimant, 160A, near the town of St Vrain, staked 11 Nov 1860
1860 Dec 6, pg 30, witness
1861 Aug 24, pg 48, witness

Mogle, V

St Vrain County Land Claims
1860 Nov 5, pg 26, Present at a meeting of the St Vrain Claim Club
1860 Nov 5, pg 27, Voter in the St Vrain Claim Club by residence
1861 Jan 10, pg 39, witness
1861 Apr 15, pg 44, land mentioned in a claim
1861 Apr 15, pg 45, buyer, for $100, land of Thomas Hollingshead

Mogle, Valentine

St Vrain County Land Claims
1861 Feb 16, pg 35, witness
1861 Feb 16, pg 36, witness
1862 [1861] Feb 16, pg 36, witness

Mogul, V

St Vrain County Land Claims
1860 Oct 23, pg 24, committee to read the reso-

lution to vacate to the
trespassers

Moir, S H
St Vrain County Land Claims
1859 Oct 6, pg 1, Present
at the first meeting of the
Citizens of Saint Vrain

Montgomery, B
St Vrain County Land Claims
1859 Sept 9, pg 4, claimant,
160A, near C P Neall's
claim, staked 9 Sept 1859

Moyers, Frank
St Vrain County Land Claims
1865 Feb 7, pg , brand filed
with the Weld County
Clerk

N

Neall, C P
St Vrain County Land Claims
1859 Sept 9, pg 3, claimant,
160A, near the Town of St
Vrain, staked 9 Sept 1859
1859 Sept 9, pg 4, witness
[1859 Oct], pg 5, seller
1859 Oct 6, pg 1, Present
at the first meeting of the
Citizens of Saint Vrain,
chosen chairman

1859 Oct 12, pg 5, claim-
ant, near St Vrain's Fort,
staked 12 Oct 1859
1860 Mar 5, pg 14, claim-
ant, 160A, near the Town
of Saint Vrain

Neall, Corydore P
St Vrain County Land Claims
1860 Mar 5, pg 13, seller,
quit claim deed to H J
Graham

Neauxhurst, George
St Vrain County Land Claims
1859 Dec 10, pg 8, witness
1860 Mar 1, pg 16, claim-
ant, 160A, improved with
a cabin built upon the
land.
1860 Apr 7, pg 16, seller,
quit claim deed to John H
Overton
1860 Apr 9, pg 17, witness

Neaxhurst, George
St Vrain County Land Claims
1859 Dec 10, pg 8, claim-
ant, 160A, staked 10 Dec
1859.
1859 Dec 15, pg 10, witness

Neill, C P
St Vrain County Land Claims
1859 Sept 9, pg 4, land
mentioned in a claim

Nuckolls, C
St Vrain County Land Claims
1859 Oct 12, pg 4, claimant,
160A, staked 12 Oct 1859
1859 Oct 12, pg 5, land
mentioned in a claim

O

Overton
St Vrain County Land Claims
1861 July 4, pg 47, land
mentioned in a claim
1861 Aug 24, pg 48, land
mentioned in a claim

Overton, H J
St Vrain County Land Claims
1862 [1861] Feb 16, pg 36,
seller

Overton, J
St Vrain County Land Claims
1861 Jan 15, pg 40, land
mentioned in a claim

Overton, J H
St Vrain County Land Claims
1859 Dec 10, pg 8, witness
1860 Nov 5, pg 26, Pres-
ent at a meeting of the St
Vrain Claim Club
1860 Nov 5, pg 27, Voter in
the St Vrain Claim Club
by residence

1860 Oct 23, pg 25, Present
at a meeting of the Saint
Vrain Claim Club, ap-
pointed to a committee to
draft rules and laws
1860 Nov 20, pg 29, witness
1861 Feb 16, pg 35, seller

Overton, John
St Vrain County Land Claims
1860 Oct 23, pg 21, Pres-
ent at a meeting of the
Citizens of St Vrain, ap-
pointed to the committee
to examin[e] the record
of the organized club of St
Vrain County

Overton, John H
St Vrain County Land Claims
1859 Dec 10, pg 8, claimant,
160A, near the Town of
Saint Vrain, staked 10 Dec
1859
1860 Apr 7, pg 16, buyer,
for $200, quit claim deed
from George Neauxhurst
1860 Apr 9, pg 17, buyer,
for $200, quit claim deed
from Burton Wakeley
1860 Aug 28, pg 19, witness
1861 Jan 10, pg 39, seller,
quit claim to Jacob Snell,
recorded at Fort Saint
Vrain
1861 Feb 16, pg 33, seller,
land to B F Reynolds

1861 Feb 16, pg 36, seller
for consideration and 100
tons of hay as security
1862 [1861] Feb 16, pg 35,
seller, to B F Reynolds

P

Packard, J B
St Vrain's Land Club Claims
1861 Feb 25, pg 6, witness,
of Montgomery Co., IA

Parker, N D
Troy District Land Claims
1860 July 17, pg 15, claimant, preemption, 160A,
SE corner of Wm H Rose's
claim
1860 Oct 11, pg 21, deed of
conveyance to Uri L Peck
1861 Aug 10, pg 7, payment
received

Patterson, James
St Vrain County Land Claims
1859 Oct 13, pg 6, claimant,
160A, near C E Miller's
claim, near J Y Jones's
claim, staked 13 Oct 1859.
1859 Oct 13, pg 6, land
mentioned in a claim

Patterson, William R
Troy District Land Claims
1860 Oct 4, pg 18, witness

Peck, Uri L
St Vrain's Land Club Claims
1861 July 31, pg 5, [witness]
Troy District Land Claims
1860 June 8, pg 13, recorder
1860 July 5, pg 13, recorder
1860 July 24, pg 14, re-
corder
1860 July 24, pg 15, re-
corder
1860 Aug 3, pg 15, recorder
1860 Aug 6, pg 16, recorder
1860 Aug 10, pg 16, re-
corder
1860 Aug 11, pg 17, re-
corder
1860 Oct 4, pg 18, paid
$250 for land of Theophi-
lus Taylor
1860 Oct 10, pg 17, re-
corder
1860 Oct 11, pg 21, re-
corder
1860 Oct 16, pg 14, re-
corder
1860 Nov 1, pg 22, recorder
1860 Dec 4, pg 22, land
mentioned in claim
1860 Dec 9, pg 22, recorder
1860 Dec 29, pg 19, re-
corder
1861 Jan 11, pg 8, recorder
1861 Jan 26, pg 19, recorder
1861 Jan 29, pg 20, recorder
1861 Jan 31, pg 11, recorder

Peck, Uri L, cont.

Troy District Land Claims

1861 Jan 31, pg 12, recorder

1861 Feb 20, pg 8, recorder

1861 Mar 17, pg 10, recorder

1861 May 22, pg 6, recorder

1861 Mar 22, pg 10, recorder

1861 Mar 28, pg 3, recorder

1861 Apr 9, pg 5, recorder

1861 Apr 30, pg 4, recorder

1861 May 29, pg 6, claimant, preemption, 160A, near C R Browne's SW corner

1861 June 17, pg 6, recorder

1861 June 22, pg 1, recorder

1861 July 1, pg 21, to pay $75 to N D Parker for land by 1 July 1861

1861 July 8, pg 1, land mentioned in claim

1861 July 9, pg 1, recorder

1861 July 10, pg 2, recorder

1861 July 18, pg 7, paid $40.65 on note dated 11 Oct 1860

1861 July 29, pg 2, recorder

1861 Aug 10, pg 7, recorder

1861 Oct 14, pg 7, recorder

Penick [Pennock] (Dwight & Pennock)

St Vrain's Land Club Claims

1861 Jan 30, pg 10, claimant, 160A, known as the Adams claim, near G E Gubins

Penick [Pennock], T R

St Vrain's Land Club Claims

1861 Jan 30, pg 10, claimant, 160A, known as the Adams claim, near G E Gubins

Pennock (Dwight & Pennock)

St Vrain's Land Club Claims

1861 Jan 30, pg 10, claimant, 160A, known as the Adams claim, near G E Gubins

Penock [Pennock] & Dwight

St Vrain's Land Club Claims

1861 Apr 11, pg 18, sellers to C C True and G W Webster

Platt River Claim Club

St Vrain County Land Claims

1861 Mar 15, pg 38, claim club mentioned in a claim

Powell, Aaron

St Vrain's Land Club Claims

1861 Feb 16, pg 32, claimant, near Jacob Bruce's claim

1861 Feb 25, pg 6, attorney, of Nebraska Territory

Powell, Anderson M
St Vrain's Land Club Claims
1861 Aug 14, pg 12, claimant, near Jacob Bruce's claim

Powell, Andrew M
St Vrain's Land Club Claims
1861 Aug 14, pg 11, claimant, near Jacob Bruce's claim
1861 Aug 19, pg 12, land mentioned in claim

Powell, D C
St Vrain's Land Club Claims
1861 Feb 25, pg 6, appoints Aaron Powell attorney, of Montgomery Co., IA
1861 May 26, pg 2, land mentioned in claim
1861 June 16, pg 7, appeared in person before Daniel Elison in Montgomery Co., IA
1861 July 24, pg 23, land mentioned in claim
1861 Aug 18, pg 15, land mentioned in claim

Powell, Mason?
St Vrain's Land Club Claims
1861 May 29, pg 4, land mentioned in claim

Putnam, George
St Vrain's Land Club Claims
1861 Aug 20, pg 13, claimant, near Aaron Runian [Runyon]'s claim
1861 Aug 20, pg 14, claimant, near Aaron Runian [Runyon]'s claim
1861 Aug 29, pg 20, claimant, near T D McClain's claim, near P White's claim
1861 Sept 8, pg 26, claimants, land known as the Bruce claim, near H Goodwin, near James G Ross
1861 Sept 8, pg 42, of Franklin Township, Jackson County, Territory of Colorado sells to Perry White land near Thomas McClain's claim, for $10

R

Rafferty, Benjamin F
St Vrain's Land Club Claims
1861 Aug 22, pg 19, claimant, near D C Taylor's claim

Randolph, S R
St Vrain County Land Claims
1861 Jan 12, pg 31, witness

Read, Luman
Franklin Township Land Claims
1860 Feb 1, pg 17, claimant, 160A, known as the Cartright claim
1860 Feb 16, pg 4, claimant, 160A

Read, Thomas
St Vrain's Land Club Claims
[1861], pg 33, buyer of the Bearman & Starns claim for $50

Read, Thomas M
St Vrain's Land Club Claims
1861 Apr 20, pg 34, claimant, 320A, near N Teter's claim, near Miles Hill's claim

Reddick, J W
St Vrain County Land Claims
1861 May 10, pg 49, buyer, quit claim from Hiram J Graham plus 49 blocks, west of Tuscarawas Street, and South of 16th Street in the Town of Saint Vrain

Reddick, J W
St Vrain County Land Claims
1860 Oct 23, pg 25, president
1860 Nov 5, pg 26, Present at a meeting of the St Vrain Claim Club

1860 Nov 5, pg 27, Voter in the St Vrain Claim Club by residence
1860 Nov 11, pg 28, witness

Reddick, Johnson W
St Vrain County Land Claims
1860 Nov 5, pg 28, claimant, 160A, about 4 miles downriver of Fort St Vrain, staked 5 Nov 1860

Reddrick, J W
St Vrain County Land Claims
1860 Oct 23, pg 25, Present at a meeting of the Saint Vrain Claim Club

Redick, J W
St Vrain County Land Claims
1860 Oct 23, pg 26, chairman

Redrick, J W
St Vrain County Land Claims
1860 Oct 23, pg 21, Present at a meeting of the Citizens of St Vrain, appointed chairman

Reed, Thomas
St Vrain's Land Club Claims
1861 Mar 29, pg 27, land mentioned in claim

Reynolds, B F
St Vrain County Land Claims
1861 Feb 16, pg 33, buyer,
for two payments of $600
each to John H Overton
1861 Feb 16, pg 36, buyer,
for 100 tons of hay cut
and stacked as surety for
the land purchase
1862 [1861] Feb 16, pg 35,
buyer, for three yokes of
oxen, one ox wagon, sev-
en cows and $1200, land
from John H Overton.
1862 [1861] Feb 16, pg 36,
buyer
1861 Aug 24, pg 48, land
mentioned in a claim
1861 Aug 24, pg 48, seller,
quit claim to James Fran-
cis

Reynolds, Frank
St Vrain County Land Claims
1860 Nov 12, pg 29, claimant, 160A, near the Town
of Saint Vrain

1861 July 4, pg 47, seller,
two claims known as the
Overton claims, near
Irish Johnny's claim, and
two claims known as the
Reynolds and Francis
claims, to George A Flem-
ing

Rhodes, J F
St Vrain County Land Claims
1860 Oct 23, pg 21, gave the
resolution in favor of H J
Graham
1860 Oct 23, pg 24, made a
motion to give notice to
the persons trespassing
on Mr Graham's claim to
leave within 24 hours
1860 Oct 23, pg 24, com-
mittee to read the reso-
lution to vacate to the
trespassers

Rice, Rufus
Troy District Land Claims
1860 Oct 16, pg 14, land of
Wm H Rose assigned to
him
1861 Feb 19, pg 8, land
mentioned in claim
1861 July 8, pg 1, claimant,
preemption, 160A
1861 July 9, pg 1, claimant
1861 July 9, pg 2, land mentioned in claim

Ripley, David
St Vrain's Land Club Claims
1861 Apr 23, pg 35, agent
1861 May 26, pg 2, surveyor
1861 June 16, pg 7, claimant, 160A, of Franklin
township, near Thomas
McClain

Ripley, David, cont.

St Vrain's Land Club Claims
1861 June 16, pg 7, agent
for Frank Ripley
1861 Sept 7, pg 44, Secretary pro tem
1861 Sept 8, pg 42, [wit-
ness]

Ripley, Frank

St Vrain's Land Club Claims
1861 Apr 23, pg 35, claimant, 160A, near Aaron
Runian [Runyan]'s claim
1861 June 16, pg 7, claimant, 160A, near Aaron
Runian [Runyan]'s claim
of 12 Nov 1860

Robenson [Robinson], James G

St Vrain's Land Club Claims
1861 Aug 28, pg 20, claimant, 160A, near Jacob
Bruce's claim

Robinson

Troy District Land Claims
1861 Jan 28, pg 11, land
mentioned in claim

Robinson, J G

Troy District Land Claims
1860 Oct 6, pg 17, land
mentioned in claim

Robinson, James G

Troy District Land Claims
1860 Oct 26, pg 22, claimant, preemption, 160A, E
of G W Coffin's SE corner

Rose, Wm H

Troy District Land Claims
1860 July 17, pg 14, claimant, preemption, 160A,
SE corner of John H R
Dunstan's claim
1860 July 17, pg 15, land
mentioned in claim
1860 Oct 11, pg 21, land
mentioned in claim

Ross, J H

St Vrain's Land Club Claims
1861 Apr 11, pg 18, witness

Ross, James C

St Vrain's Land Club Claims
1861 Nov 21, pg 39, land
mentioned in claim

Ross, James G

St Vrain's Land Club Claims
1861 Aug 14, pg 11, land
mentioned in claim

Roues, J F

St Vrain County Land Claims
1860 Oct 23, pg 21, Pres-
ent at a meeting of the
Citizens of St Vrain, ap-
pointed to the committee
to examin[e] the record

of the organized club of St
Vrain County

Ruby, Orin G
St Vrain County Land Claims
1861 Jan 18, pg 40, claimant, 160A, near Jacob
Snell's claim

Runian [Runyan]
St Vrain's Land Club Claims
1861 Apr 17, pg 28, land
mentioned in claim

Runian [Runyan], Aaron
St Vrain's Land Club Claims
1861 Feb 2, pg 10, land
mentioned in claim
1861 Apr 23, pg 35, land
mentioned in claim
1861 May 17, pg 36, land
mentioned in claim
1861 June 16, pg 7, land
mentioned in claim
1861 Aug 20, pg 14, land
mentioned in claim

Runian [Runyan], G S
St Vrain's Land Club Claims
1861 Sept 8, pg 26, land
mentioned in claim

Runyan, J S
Franklin Township Land Claims
1860 June 30, pg 8, claimant, 2 miles above Wilson
Stanley Ranch

S

Sage & Beckwith
Franklin Township Land Claims
1860 July 10, pg 5, claimants, near Jese [Jesse]
Bloodsworth's SE corner

Saint Vrain Town Site
St Vrain County Land Claims
[1859 Oct], pg 5, town
mentioned in a claim
1859 Sept 9, pg 4, town
mentioned in a claim

Sanders, B
St Vrain's Land Club Claims
1861 June 24, pg 9, claimant, 160A, near D H
Taylor's claim
1861 June 24, pg 10, claimant, 160A, near D H
Taylor's claim

Sanders, Barcley
St Vrain's Land Club Claims
1861 Aug 19, pg 13, claimant, near T J Taylor's
claim

Saville, John J
St Vrain County Land Claims
1861 May 3, pg 42, buyer,
for $100, land of S F
Mitchell near Fort
Vasques

Saville, John J, cont.

St Vrain County Land Claims
1861 May 3, pg 43, buyer, for $100, land of S F Mitchell near Fort Vasques

Scott, John

St Vrain's Land Club Claims
1861 Dec 1, pg 38, claimants, 160A, near Elizabeth Day's claim

Scourfield, Wm

St Vrain County Land Claims
1858 Nov 1, pg 18, claimant, 160A, a log cabin was erected on 1 Nov 1858, claim renewed and staked 10 May 1860

Smead, C L

Troy District Land Claims
1861 Apr 30, pg 4, claimant, preemption, 160A, near G W Coffin's NE corner, and 30A, SW corner of Thomas Dunn's claim

Smith, A H

St Vrain County Land Claims
1860 Nov 5, pg 27, Voter in the St Vrain Claim Club by residence
1861 Mar 15, pg 38, land mentioned in a claim
1861 Mar 15, pg 39, witness

Smith, Andrew H

St Vrain County Land Claims
1861 Mar 15, pg 38, claimant, 160A, near the cabin in which he resides recorded in the Platt River Claim Club on 22 June 1860
[1861 Mar], pg 41, buyer, quit claim from Franklin Finney, near Geo Lyche's claim

Smith, J H T

St Vrain's Land Club Claims
1861 Nov 21, pg 39, claimant, near James C Ross's claim

Smith, Jas H Thos

St Vrain's Land Club Claims
1861 Nov 28, pg 43, witness

Smith, Michal

St Vrain County Land Claims
[1861 Mar], pg 41, buyer, quit claim from Franklin Finney, near Geo Lyche's claim

Smith, Michoe

St Vrain County Land Claims
1861 Mar 15, pg 38, claimant, 160A, near A H Smith's claim, staked 22 June 1860 and have resided on the land since that time

Smith, Mr
St Vrain County Land Claims
1860 Nov 5, pg 27, Voter in the St Vrain Claim Club by residence

Smith, S H
St Vrain County Land Claims
1860 Oct 23, pg 21, Present at a meeting of the Citizens of St Vrain, appointed Secretary
1860 Oct 23, pg 21, Present at a meeting of the Citizens of St Vrain, appointed to the committee to examin[e] the record of the organized club of St Vrain County
1860 Oct 23, pg 24, committee to read the resolution to vacate to the trespassers
1860 Oct 23, pg 25, secretary
1860 Oct 23, pg 25, Present at a meeting of the Saint Vrain Claim Club, appointed to a committee to draft rules and laws

Smith, William
St Vrain's Land Club Claims
1862, Jan 26, pg 40, claimant, 160A, near Thomas McClain's claim

Snell, J
St Vrain County Land Claims
1861 Jan 12, pg 31, witness

Snell, Jacob
St Vrain County Land Claims
1861 Jan 10, pg 39, buyer, for $100, quit claim deed from John H Overstreet
1861 Jan 15, pg 40, claimant, 160A, near J Overton's old claim, staked and improved 15 Jan 1861
1861 Jan 18, pg 40, land mentioned in a claim
1861 Jan 18, pg 40, witness

St Vrain's Fort
St Vrain County Land Claims
1859 Oct 12, pg 5, fort mentioned in a claim

Stanley, G B
St Vrain's Land Club Claims
1861 Apr 11, pg 29, land mentioned in claim

Stanley, W
Franklin Township Land Claims
1860 Feb 12, pg 1, agent for N Wisner
1860 June 24, pg 5, recorder

Stanley, Wilson
Franklin Township Land Claims
1860 Feb 12, pg 2, claimant,
NW corner of B A Frank-
lin, 80A and south of John
Weese, 40A
1860 June 30, pg 8, ranch
mentioned in claim

Starns, B H
St Vrain's Land Club Claims
[1861], pg 34, seller to
Thomas Read

Starns, Byron H
St Vrain's Land Club Claims
[1861], pg 33, selling their
claim to Thomas Read

Steck, James
St Vrain County Land Claims
1859 Oct 6, pg 1, Present
at the first meeting of the
Citizens of Saint Vrain

Stone, Louis
St Vrain's Land Club Claims
1861 Mar 25, pg 26, land
mentioned in claim

Sulfer Spring Ranch
St Vrain's Land Club Claims
1860 Feb 2, pg 41, land
mentioned in claim

Swallow, Isaac
St Vrain's Land Club Claims
1861 Aug 29, pg 19, claimant, near W R Blawer
[Blore]'s claim
1861 Sept 8, pg 26, claimant, changes the boundar-
ies of his claim, near G S
Runian [Runyan]

T

Taxel [Traxel], John [Jonathan]
Franklin Township Land Claims
1860 Feb 16, pg 4, claimant,
between Baker and Lum
Read, 160A

Taylor & Carter
St Vrain's Land Club Claims
1861 Apr 7, pg 28, claim-
ants, have built a dam,
and commenced building
a ditch with 14 square feet
of running water, with
each party entitled to
water from the ditch

Taylor, D C
St Vrain's Land Club Claims
1860 Oct 29, pg 16, claimant, land known as the
Adams claim, near Gwin's
line
1861 Apr 7, pg 28, claim-
ants, have built a dam,

and commenced building a ditch with 14 square feet of running water, with each party entitled to water from the ditch
1861 Aug 22, pg 19, land mentioned in claim
[1861], pg 34, witness

Taylor, D H
St Vrain's Land Club Claims
1861 June 23, pg 9, claimant, 160A, near H Goodwin's claim, and G James's claim
1861 June 24, pg 9, land mentioned in claim

Taylor, David C
Franklin Township Land Claims
1860 June 26, pg 7, claimant, corner of Wm Baker
1860 June 26, pg 18, claimant, near Mr Baker's claim
1861 May 21, pg 1, land mentioned in claim
1861 May 26, pg 2, claimant, 160A, near Dr H Goodwin's claim, and D C Powell's claim

Taylor, Phizer G
St Vrain's Land Club Claims
1861 May 21, pg 1, claimant, 160A, near Daniel C Taylor's claim

Taylor, T J
St Vrain's Land Club Claims
1861 Aug 19, pg 12, claimant, near R S Low's claim
1861 Aug 19, pg 13, land mentioned in claim
1861 Aug 19, pg 13, claimant, Near R S Low's claim

Taylor, Theophilus
Troy District Land Claims
1860 June 8, pg 13, claimant, preemption, 160A, W of A N Allen's SE corner
1860 Oct 4, pg 18, deed of conveyance to Uri L Peck
1861 Mar 28, pg 3, land mentioned in claim
1861 July 29, pg 2, land mentioned in claim

Taylor, Thomas
St Vrain's Land Club Claims
1861 July 31, pg 5, [witness]

Taylor, W J
St Vrain's Land Club Claims
1861 Apr 1, pg 27, claimant, near Miles Hill's claim

Taylor, Warren
St Vrain's Land Club Claims
1861 July 31, pg 5, [witness]
1861 Oct 14, pg 7, claimant, preemption, 160A, north of C R Brown's SW corner

Teater, N
St Vrain's Land Club Claims
1861 Apr 8, pg 23, land
mentioned in claim

Teater, Wesly [Wesley]
Franklin Township Land Claims
1860 June 30, pg 7, claimant, near a spring north
side of St Vrain Creek

Teter, N
St Vrain's Land Club Claims
1861 Apr 20, pg 34, land
mentioned in claim

Thomas, Mr
St Vrain County Land Claims
1860 Oct 23, pg 21, Pres-
ent at a meeting of the
Citizens of St Vrain, ap-
pointed to the committee
to examin[e] the record
of the organized club of St
Vrain County

Thorn, A
St Vrain County Land Claims
1860 Oct 23, pg 25, Present
at a meeting of the Saint
Vrain Claim Club
1860 Oct 23, pg 26, secretary
1860 Nov 5, pg 26, Pres-
ent at a meeting of the St
Vrain Claim Club

Thorn, Albert
St Vrain County Land Claims
1860 Aug 28, pg 19, claimant, 160A, near the Town
of Saint Vrain, staked 28
Aug 1860
1860 Nov 5, pg 27, Voter in
the St Vrain Claim Club
by residence
1861 Feb 4, pg 32, land
mentioned in a claim

Titus, J A
Troy District Land Claims
1861 Jan 28, pg 12, claimant, 158A, NE corner of
Henry Daniel's claim
1861 Jan 31, pg 11, witness

Tower, G
St Vrain's Land Club Claims
1861 May 20, pg 37, land
mentioned in claim

Tower, Gilbert
St Vrain's Land Club Claims
1861 Apr 11, pg 18, witness
1861 Apr 11, pg 29, witness

Tower, J
St Vrain's Land Club Claims
1861 July 29, pg 11,
rec[order]

Town of Saint Vrain
St Vrain County Land Claims
1861 May 10, pg 49, town
mentioned in a claim

1859 Sept 9, pg 3, town mentioned in a claim
1859 Oct 12, pg 11, town mentioned in a claim
1859 Dec 10, pg 8, town mentioned in a claim
1860 Jan 7, pg 9, town mentioned in a claim
1860 Feb 21, pg 12, town mentioned in a claim
1860 Oct, pg 21, Platt [Plat] recorded for the town of Saint Vrain
1860 Nov 12, pg 29, town mentioned in a claim
1861 Feb 4, pg 33, town mentioned in a claim

Traxel, Johnathan
St Vrain's Land Club Claims
1860 Feb 15, pg 16, claimant, 160A, near Richard Gwin's claim, and John T Burch's claim, is known as the Cartwright claim
1860 Feb 15, pg 17, claimant, 160A, near Richard Gwin's claim, and John T Burch's claim, is known as the Cartwright claim

Traxel, Jonathan
Franklin Township Land Claims
1860 Feb 15, pg 3, claimant, east of Richard Gaines, west of John T Burch, 160A

Trowbridge, Geo
St Vrain County Land Claims
1859 Oct 6, pg 1, Present at the first meeting of the Citizens of Saint Vrain

True, C C
St Vrain's Land Club Claims
1861 Apr 11, pg 18, buyers of land owned by Pennock & Dwight, in Franklin District, known as the Adams claim, near G C Gwin

Tucker, J H
St Vrain's Land Club Claims
1860 Feb 2, pg 41, claimant, 160A, known as Sulfer? Spring Ranch

V

Vasques, A P
St Vrain County Land Claims
1859 Oct 28, pg 7, land mentioned in a claim

Vasques, Louis
St Vrain County Land Claims
1859 Oct 28, pg 7, claimant, 160A, near A P Vasques's claim

Vasquez, A P
St Vrain County Land Claims
1859 Oct 28, pg 7, claimant, 160A, near old Fort Vasques

W

Wagner, T F
Franklin Township Land Claims
1860 June 25, pg 6, [agent for D C Hoover]

Wakely, Burton
St Vrain County Land Claims
1860 Mar 1, pg 17, claimant, 160A, near the Town Site of St Vrain, staked 1 Mar 1860, improved with a good log cabin.
1860 Apr 9, pg 17, seller, quit claim deed to John H Overton

Wallrod, A
St Vrain County Land Claims
1859 Oct 12, pg 5, claimant, 160A, near C Nuckolls's claim, staked 12 Oct 1859

Waterloo
St Vrain's Land Club Claims
1861 Aug 19, pg 12, town site mentioned in claim

Wayne, Wm
Troy District Land Claims
1861 Mar 28, pg 3, claimant, preemption, 160A, SE corner of Theophilus Taylor claim

Webster, G W
St Vrain's Land Club Claims
1861 Apr 11, pg 18, buyers of land owned by Pennock & Dwight, in Franklin District, known as the Adams claim, near G C Gwin

Weemott [Wemott], S S
St Vrain's Land Club Claims
1861 Aug 27, pg 21, claimant, 160A, near T D McClain's claim

Wees [Weese], Columbus
St Vrain's Land Club Claims
1862, Jan 23, pg 40, claimant, near N Wisner's claim

Weese, John
Franklin Township Land Claims
1860 Feb 12, pg 2, claimant, NW corner of B A Franklin
1860 Feb 12, pg 2, land mentioned in claim

White, P
St Vrain's Land Club Claims
1861 Aug 29, pg 20, land
mentioned in claim

White, Perry
St Vrain's Land Club Claims
1861 Feb 16, pg 29, claimant, 160A,
1861 May 17, pg 2, agent
1861 May 17, pg 36, claimant, 160A, near Aaron
Runian [Runyon]'s claim
recorded on 1 Nov 1861
[1860], near T D Mc-
Clain's claim
1861 May 18, pg 36, agent
1861 Sept 8, pg 42, buyer,
land from George Putnam
1861 Nov 8, pg 39, land
mentioned in claim
1861 Nov 28, pg 43, of
Boulder County, Colo-
rado Territory, sells land
near Thomas McClain for
$200 to J N Hollowell

Williams, D H
St Vrain County Land Claims
1860 Mar 5, pg 13, witness

Williams, Scott
St Vrain County Land Claims
1861 Jan 27, pg 31, claimant, 160A, staked 27 Jan
1861

Wisner [Weisner], Norman
Franklin Township Land Claims
1860 Feb 12, pg 1, claim-
ant, south of B A Frank-
lin's claim, south of Wm
Baker's claim, 160A

Wisner, N
St Vrain's Land Club Claims
1862, Jan 23, pg 40, land
mentioned in claim

Wogen
St Vrain County Land Claims
1861 Feb 16, pg 34, land
mentioned in a claim

Wogin, John
St Vrain County Land Claims
1861 Aug 24, pg 48, land
mentioned in a claim
1860 Nov 20, pg 29, claimant, 160A

Wood, William
St Vrain's Land Club Claims
1861 May 23, pg 41, claimant, of Franklin Town-
ship, 160A, near Dr H
Goodwin's claim

Z

Zurick [Zweck], George

St Vrain's Land Club Claims

1861 Aug 11, pg 14, claimant, of Franklin Township, 160A, 1 mile north of Jacob Bruce's claim as filed on 18 June 1860

1861 Aug 11, pg 15, claimant, of Franklin Township, 160A, 1 mile north of Jacob Bruce's claim as filed on 18 June 1860

Additional Colorado Research Titles

If you borrowed this copy from a library and would like to order a copy, please send a check or money order to: Iron Gate Publishing, P.O. Box 999, Niwot, CO 80544. Our books are available online to institutions through Lightning Source, to individuals at Amazon.com and on our website:

www.irongate.com

Boulder City Town Company Lot Sales 1859-1864: An Annotated Map Guide
ISBN 978-1-879579-87-3 $15.95 + $4.00 S&H

Brainard's Hotel Register, Boulder, Colorado, 1880: An Annotated Index
ISBN 978-1-879579-86-6 $15.95 $5.00 S&H

Boulder County Commissioner's Journal, 1861-1871: An Annotated Transcription
ISBN 978-1-879579-77-4 $45.99 + $5.00 S&H

Boulder County Commissioners Journal, 1871-1874: An Annotated Transcription
ISBN 978-1-879579-91-0 $39.95 + $5.00 S&H

Brainard Hotel Register, 6 March-18 December 1880: An Annotated Index
ISBN 978-1-879579-86-6, $15.95 + $5.00

Colorado's Territorial Masons: An An'notated Index of the Proceedings of the Grand Lodge of Colorado, 1861–1876
ISBN 978-1-879579-85-9 $29.95 + $5.00 S&H

Boulder, Colorado Teachers, 1878-1900: An Annotated Index
ISBN 978-1-879579-93-4 $11.95 + $4.00 S&H

Boulder County, Colorado District Court Execution Docket, 1875-1885: An An'd Index
ISBN 978-1-879579-94-1 $11.95 + $4.00 S&H

Denver, Colorado Police Force Record, 1879-1903: An Annotated Index
ISBN 978-1-879579-81-1 $11.95 + $4.00 S&H

Boulder, Colorado Births 1892–1906: An Annotated Index
ISBN 978-1-879579-79-8 $11.95 + $4.00 S&H

Arapahoe County, Colorado Territory Criminal Court Index, 1862-1879: An An'd Index
ISBN 978-1-879579-70-5 $11.95 + $4.00 S&H

Boulder County Probate Court Appraisement Record A, 1875-1888: An Annotated Index
ISBN 978-1-879579-72-9 $11.95 + $4.00 S&H

Boulder County Assessor's Tax List, 1875: An Annotated Index
ISBN 978-1-879579-55-2 $11.95 + $4.00 S&H

Boulder County Assessor's Tax List, 1876: An Annotated Index
ISBN 978-1-879579-56-9 $11.95 + $4.00 S&H

Boulder Valley Presbyterian Church Records, 1863-1900: An Annotated Index
ISBN 978-1-879579-58-3 $11.95 + $4.00 S&H

Boulder's Masonic Pioneers, 1867-1886: Members of Columbia Lodge No. 14, Boulder County, Colorado Territory
ISBN 978-1-879579-57-6 $15.95 + $4.00 S&H

Publishing Titles

If you would like to order one of these books, please send a check or money order to: Iron Gate Publishing, P.O. Box 999, Niwot, CO 80544. Our books are available online to institutions through Lightning Source, to individuals at Amazon.com and on our website:

www.irongate.com

Set Yourself Up to Self-Publish: A Genealogist's Guide
      ISBN 978-1-879579-99-6 $19.95 + $5.00 S&H

Publish Your Genealogy: A Step-by-Step Guide for Preserving Your Research for the Next Generation
      ISBN 978-1-879579-62-0 $24.95 + $5.00 S&H

Publish Your Family History: A Step-by-Step Guide to Writing the Stories of Your Ancestors
      ISBN 978-1-879579-63-7 $24.95 + $5.00 S&H

Publish a Local History: A Step-by-Step Guide from Finding the Right Project to Finished Book
      ISBN 978-1-879579-64-4 $24.95 + $5.00 S&H

Publish a Memoir: A Step-by-Step Guide to Saving Your Memories for Future Generations
      ISBN 978-1-879579-65-1 $24.95 + $5.00 S&H

Publish a Biography: A Step-by-Step Guide to Capturing the Life and Times of an Ancestor or a Generation
      ISBN 978-1-879579-66-8 $24.95 + $5.00 S&H

Publish a Photo Book: A Step-by-Step Guide for Transforming Your Genealogical Research into a Stunning Family Heirloom
      ISBN 978-1-879579-67-5 $24.95 + $5.00 S&H

Publish a Source Index: A Step-by-Step Guide to Creating a Genealogically Useful Index, Abstract or Transcription
      ISBN 978-1-879579-68-2 $24.95 + $5.00 S&H

Publish Your Specialty: A Step-by-Step Guide for Imparting Your Research Expertise to Others
      ISBN 978-1-879579-76-7 $24.95 + $5.00 S&H

www.ingramcontent.com/pod-product-compliance
Lightning Source LLC
Chambersburg PA
CBHW061516040426
42450CB00008B/1644